I LIKE THAT STUFF

poems from many cultures
selected by
MORAG STYLES

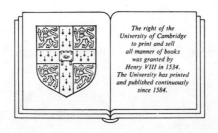

The right of the
University of Cambridge
to print and sell
all manner of books
was granted by
Henry VIII in 1534.
The University has printed
and published continuously
since 1584.

CAMBRIDGE UNIVERSITY PRESS

Cambridge

New York   New Rochelle

Melbourne   Sydney

for Ross
who likes poetry too,
but not as much as football . . .

I am grateful to Adrian Mitchell for letting me use the refrain from his poem 'I Like That Stuff' for my title. The full poem appears in Adrian Mitchell 'POEMS' published by Jonathan Cape.

Published by the Press Syndicate of the University of Cambridge
The Pitt Building, Trumpington Street, Cambridge CB2 1RP
32 East 57th Street, New York, NY 10022, USA
10 Stamford Road, Oakleigh, Melbourne 3166, Australia

First published 1984
Fourth printing 1987

Printed in Great Britain at the University Press, Cambridge

ISBN 0 521 25662 3 hard covers
ISBN 0 521 27637 3 paperback

Illustrations by Joanne Smith and Bernard Georges

PTL

Contents

An asterisk indicates that the poem has been written by a young person

Introduction

●

Each time I poem with children I find myself along that high tension
wire that is their sense of shape and sound and motion having to go back
swept back by them really to the very shores and sources of the poem: to
the colours of the first sun rising the song of the first sea's salt giving us
our blood that hool we stoop into and call a tent or playground wigwam
knowing it is womb and wound and bleeding egg of nebulae. So that
when Morag ask the iani to write an introduction to her breeve of poems
i knew i couldn't do it Or rather i would have to wait and chop it down
like firewood; that i would have no type to light that kind of fire; would
have to learn again which stick of word to rub what flint of primal
metaphor to crack alight i lines. I also knew I could not write it by i-self.
Children's poems and the best poems for children (not quite the same
thing but they come from the same moving shallows of the cave) are if
anything social communal tribal: we chant enact we signify: spider
tarbaby jabberwocky nnurn pacman beanstalk RTD-2 And Morag
celebrates all this she gathers it and brings it out like harvest: not English
poem only lonely as has too long & often been the case but the whole
wide wonderful world that is the heritage of 'princess margaret english'
and all us thrilldren. John Agard's limbo man is here and Soussou
moons, a 'cloud-cat lapping there on high' from India, messages from
Kofi Awoonor Ghana China Japan and Australasia. And so is not only
dwarfs & giants, elegies & elves & daffodils we give you now but man
and mama grandma's spells magic & a whole set a different drummers
and bandana butterflies and there is water everywhere and ears to hear
that earth is made of heaven as it is of earth and the cow still jump over
the spoon. So that with all this real already here that dream so nearly
there I could not right the Introduction. Didn't need to. Simply had to
join in. But wait! Don't take it haul for granted! *Poem isn't no freeness!*
Like the man said *I mean it never was no swich-on switch off t'ing like
TV.* And so i wrote this poem: i-man initiation song for Morag Styles
anthology.

THE MANAGEMENT WILL NOT RESPONSIBLE THIS BOOK IF YOU
DONOT GO THROUGH THESE PORTICOES/OKAY?

4

INITIATION POEM FOR MORAG STYLES ANTHOLOGY
to be performed in inity before entering the flattened fifth

form first the circle and listen
-
let your hands touch the hands in the round and sit
slowly
sinking slowly into the ground with your feet
crossed and your arms
warmly
-
make a book of the palms of your hands and read the prayers there
and listen to the same seas
close your eyes for a while and watch the stars open your eyes
when you hear that distant sun call your name
-
say your name soft
to the poet who lives to the left of your heart in the sunlight beside you
let him say let her say his name say her name to the name who sits to the
    left of its shadow
let each name let each name slowly circle the world on its whispering wave-
    length tidal
round time and then let it stop where it started
-
now each name is a pebble or coin or rain-
drop dropp-
ing into the pool
-
is it green
that you harp

is it harp-
oon blue

will the
names dance for you

rub-a-dub-dub
and then *do*

it again

•

now the names belong to us all
and the sound that is sound that is silence is tall

•

the sky is no wall at all

•

so slowly
my sisteren

drum
drum
druminit

slowly
slowly
ever so slowly

my brederen

druminit
druminit
drumminit

close the stares of your eyes till they touch the trickle of wind on your face

do
you feel

do
you feel

it/don't
touch

it/just

let it syllable there
like the wind in the palms of your hand-

claps/
look

like the word on the edge of your poem

•

breathe the poem   Edward Kamau Brathwaite

Me, Myself and Others

When you meet your friend,
your face brightens —
you have struck gold.

Kassia, 9th Century
Greece

With clothes the new are best;
with friends the old are best.

traditional
China

1 **Me**

You got no right
to look at me,
There might be things
I don't want you to see.
Things I need
to hide
behind this mask,
my face.

Deepak Kalha*
U.K.

2 It is impossible
   for anyone to enter
   our small world.
   The adults don't
   understand us
   they think
   we're childish.
   No one can get in
   our world.
   It has a wall twenty feet high
   and adults
   have only ten feet ladders.

Ross Falconer*
Australia

3 get under the covers
   pull up my feet
   and stick out
   my tongue
   at nobody

Ishikawa Takuboku
Japan

4 I am

I am a human being, a boy.
You may say I am a special compound which can
Think, can see . . . etc,
And a little bit different from cat, dog, etc.
You may say I am a body with a soul
which is living.
I have a special computer which requires no electricity.
It is in my skull.
It works all the time until night.
When it can't work, I can't work.
I have a special pump which pumps the blood all over
my body, and no electricity required.
It is in my left chest,
But it never stops or feels tired.
When it stops, I stop.
I have some other machines which require no electricity
And they never stop or feel tired.
But when they stop, I stop.
That's me.

However, I am still I!

Chun Po Man*
Hong Kong

9

5   I am black as I thought
My lids are as brown as
I thought
My hair is curled as I
thought
I am free as I know.

Accabre Huntley*
U.K.

6 **Blackness**

Blackness is me,
For I am black.
What mundane pow'r can change that fact?
If I should roam the world afar;
If I should soar the heights of stars;
If earthly honours I attract,
I'd still be black—
For black is black
And there is naught can change that fact.
Africa's my mother's name;
And it is she from whence I came.
That's why I'm black,
For so is she.
Blackness is our identity.
Blackness is what we want to be.
You are white;
Whiteness is you.
My Africa is not your mother,
But yet you are — you are my brother!

Glyne Walrond
Caribbean

10

7 Happy Birthday, Dilroy!

My name is Dilroy.
I'm a little black boy
and I'm eight today.

My birthday cards say
it's great to be eight
and they sure right
coz I got a pair of skates
I want for a long time.

My birthday cards say,
Happy Birthday, Dilroy!
But, Mummy, tell me why
they don't put a little boy
that looks a bit like me.
Why the boy on the card so white?

John Agard
U.K.

The Travelling Boy

Hot leaf-curling sun
Gold glistening wings of
Vivid butterflies among
The river peppermint.

Across the sky of
Bobbing thistledown,
Young swallows in their
First freedom fly.

The shoals of tiny fish
Have thinned, those left
Are now a finger long,
Wise and self-assured.

The boy sits fishing,
All thoughts but one
Lost amid the reeds;
Like any other boy.

His rod is a hazel wand,
His line, old rick-twine
His hook, a rusty safety-pin,
But the day . . . the day is HIS.

Beshlie Heron
Romany/U.K.

9 Sometimes

Sometimes
when I'm the only child
in the company of grown-ups
I feel so bored
like a pussycat I feel
all alone
and then I wish I had
a ball of wool to play with

Lesley Miranda*
U.K.

10 Stevie

Stevie pelting Ma Rose mango
With his good friend Hicks
Even though his mother tell him
He would get some licks.

Stevie pick up a big boulder
And he aim with zest
What he thought was Julie mango
Was a big jap nest.

The japs start swarming Stevie head
And he start to squeal
His mother said, 'I tired tell you
Who don't hear does feel.'

Odette Thomas
Caribbean

14

11 Mothers

One thing about Mothers –
                    They never stop talking.
As soon as they
             start talking to a friend
             It's hours before
                        they stop.

When I go to shop
                With my mum
I always
      have to
           carry the load.

I bet it's
      the same with
           all the others.

Marisa Horsford*
U.K.

12 Granny Granny Please Comb My Hair

Granny Granny
please comb my hair
you always take your time
you always take such care

You put me to sit on a cushion
between your knees
you rub a little coconut oil
parting gentle as a breeze

Mummy Mummy
she's always in a hurry–hurry
rush
she pulls my hair
sometimes she tugs

But Granny
you have all the time in the world
and when you're finished
you always turn my head and say
'Now who's a nice girl.'

Grace Nichols
U.K.

13 In trouble

Whoever is caught
I get the blame
Wherever you go
I get into trouble.
If Tom and I was fighting
And get caught,
I will be the one to get into trouble,
And Tom gets a big cuddle.
It encourages him to do it again and again,
Even over the dinner table.
Whoever is naughty
I get the blame
And they get the cuddle.

Vivian Usherwood*
U.K.

14 Richard's Brother Speaks

Richard . . .
What's the matter? Why you not smiln' no more?
You wretch, you bruk the window?
Daddy a go peel you 'kin,
'Im a go peel it like how he peel orange.
When Daddy come true dat door.
You better run.
You better leave de country!
'im a-go peel you 'kin.
You bottom a go warm tonight though!
Me goin' cook dinner pon you backside
When 'im done wid you
Richard 'im a come!
Run, bwoy, run!

Desmond Strachan*
U.K.

15   from **Banza**

How yu mean
Banza break he foot?
He what? been in fire again?
Ah know it, ah know it.
Ah always say it bound to happen.
Ah caution him time an time again,
Leave de people fire alone,
But he can' hear.
Like he have hot-foot.
Every fire in town, he dey.
He can't hear siren blow,
But is gone he gone.
De man always chasin' fire-brigade.
If he like fire so much,
Why he dont turn fire-man?
Eh? Yu tell me dat?
If fire in de country, Banza dey
If fire in de town, Banza dey
Anywhere dey have fire, Banza dey.
How he break de foot?
He what? He fall off de roof?
Yu mean Banza been on de roof?
He been what? helpin' dem hold hose?
Now yu ehn see he mad?
What he doin' on de people roof?

Paul Keens-Douglas
Caribbean

Fun and Games

Cockroach noh gat no business
eena cock fight!

Barbara Zencraft
Caribbean

A dragon stranded in shallow water
furnishes amusement for the shrimps

traditional
China

16 **Finger Game**

This one says: hunter is biting me.
This one says: Mother is not at home.
This one says: let's go to the farm and steal.
This one says: and if the farmer catches us?
This one says: go and steal; I'll stand apart.

from the Yoruba
Translated by U. Beier
Africa

17 **Riddles**

Two tiny birds jump over two hundred trees.
The black one is squatting – the red one is licking his bottom.
A round calabash in the spear grass.
A thin staff reaches from heaven to earth.

from the Yoruba
Translated by U. Beier
Africa

18 **Riddle me-ree**

You cannot hold it more than a minute
Though it is lighter than a feather.

Here's a thing:
Sixteen working,
Sixteen resting,
Two shepherds,
Two listeners,
And one a-stare.

traditional
Translated A. Arberry
Malta

Solutions to riddles on p.93

19 Children in this home do not like me

Children in this home do not like me,
I like fighting;
Children in this home do not like me,
I like fighting;
When my mother goes to the well,
I like fighting;
When my mother goes to collect firewood,
I like fighting;
When my mother goes to weed the garden,
I like fighting;
Children in this home do not like me,
I like fighting.

Okot p'Bitek
Africa

20 Yellow Butter

Yellow butter purple jelly red jam black bread
Spread it thick
Say it quick
Yellow butter purple jelly red jam black bread
Spread it thicker
Say it quicker
Yellow butter purple jelly red jam black bread
Now repeat it
While you eat it
Yellow butter purple jelly red jam black bread
Don't talk with your mouth full!

Mary Ann Hoberman
U.S.A.

21 YOU!

You!
Your head is like a hollow drum.
You!
Your eyes are like balls of flame.
You!
Your ears are like fans for blowing fire.
You!
Your nostril is like a mouse's hole.
You!
Your mouth is like a lump of mud.
You!
Your hands are like drum-sticks.
You!
Your belly is like a pot of bad water.
You!
Your legs are like wooden posts.
You!
Your backside is like a mountain-top.

from the Igbo
Africa

22 Shirley Said

Who wrote 'kick me' on my back?
Who put a spider in my mack?
Who's the one who pulls my hair?
Tries to trip me everywhere?
Who runs up to me and strikes me?
That boy there – I think he likes me.

Dennis Doyle
U.K.

23 Curse

ON A DRIVER
WHO SPLASHED HIS NEW PANTS
WHEN HE COULD
HAVE JUST AS EASILY
DRIVEN
AROUND THE PUDDLE

May your large intestine freeze in a knot like a skate-lace!
May manhole covers collapse wherever you go.
May garbage strikes pester your street, and may you
grow eight new
Feet and get poison ivy on every toe!

Dennis Lee
Canada

from **Insec' Lesson**

Todder nite mi a watch one program,
Yuh did watch it to Miss Vie?
De one wid de whole heap o'ants an' bug,
Mi couldn' believe mi yeye

When mi see ow de ants dem lib
An hep out one anedda,
So much hundred tousan ants
Dey wuk an' pull togedda.

De mooma ants she big an fat
So she liddung lay egg all day.
De solja ants tan up guard de door,
Mek sure no enemy no come dem way.

De worka ants a de bessis one,
Dem always wuk togedda
Fi feed de queen, an store de eggs,
An wash dem likkle bredda.

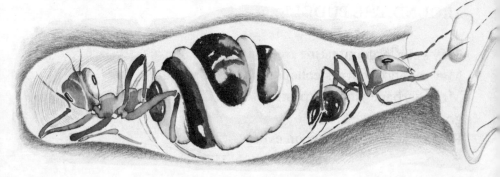

Some go out fi gadda food
Fi feed dose in de nes'
Some a dig hole fi mek new room
An some clean up de mess.

I' please mi fi see ow de ants dem pull,
An try fi get tings done,
Dem wuk an eat an sleep togedda
An a not even dem one.

Far mi see whole heap o' odda insect
Wasp, bug an fly an bee,
All a wuk togedda
Ina perfec' harmony.

Valerie Bloom
U.K.

25   In Praise of Noses

Not exactly ornamental
even when quite straight,
these funny, two-holed things!

But think:
if they faced upwards
they'd blow hats off

when one sneezed
and fill with rain
when it poured.

If sideways,
what objects of derision
snuff-takers would be!

Now all that a sneeze merits
is a 'God bless'.

God bless indeed, sweet nose,
warming, filtering,

humidifying the air as I breathe,
you do a marvellous job!

Prabhu S. Guptara
U.K.

26 Have You Ever Seen?

Have you ever seen
a blue tadpole
Have you ever seen
a spoilt-brat toad

Have you ever seen
a walking fish
Have you ever seen
a grunting chick

Have you ever seen
a singing spider
Have you ever seen
a dancing tiger

Have you ever seen
a monkey swimming
Have you ever seen
a turtle grinning

Have you ever?

Grace Nichols
U.K.

27 **Reasons for Extinction**

Dodos do
nothing to
dastards who
do dodos down.

Dog-god does
not defend
dodos being
undone.

Dodos lovey-dovey
with dodo darlings
don't become
dodo dams or dads.

Dodos do
dumb things
like Dido or
dinosaurs did.

So dodos die
out.

H. O. Nazareth
U.K.

Painting the Gate

I painted the mailbox. That was fun.
I painted it postal blue.
Then I painted the gate.
I painted a spider that got on the gate.
I painted his mate.
I painted the ivy around the gate.
Some stones I painted blue,
and part of the cat as he rubbed by.
I painted my hair. I painted my shoe.
I painted the slats, both front and back,
all their bevelled edges too.
I painted the numbers on the gate —
I shouldn't have, but it was too late.
I painted the posts, each side and top,
I painted the hinges, the handle, the lock,
several ants and a moth asleep in a crack.
At last I was through.
I'd painted the gate
shut, me out, with both hands dark blue,
as well as my nose, which,
early on, because of a sudden itch,
got painted. But wait!
I had painted the gate.

May Swenson
U.S.A.

29 Throw the Ball

Let's throw the ball at the sun,
Make it laugh and sigh,
See it hide and smile and run,
Then fall from the evening sky.

Let's throw the ball at the moon,
And watch it falling down,
Then catch it with a silver spoon
In the middle of the town.

Edwin Thumboo
Singapore

30 **Little One, Lately**

Little one, lately
When you come to me,
In the bed there seem
Not two, but three.

The third one, this stranger
On your other side,
Has a burglar's eyes,
Where shall we hide?

He has cracked privacy
And flashes the sun
On us, like a torch,
Little one, little one.

All your grey secrets
Scurrying in the next
Room, none may see,
But the wind shall guess.

No, no, I love you.
Do not cry. Please.
What I just said
Was merely to tease.

Taufiq Rafat
Pakistan

Birds, Beasts and Butterflies

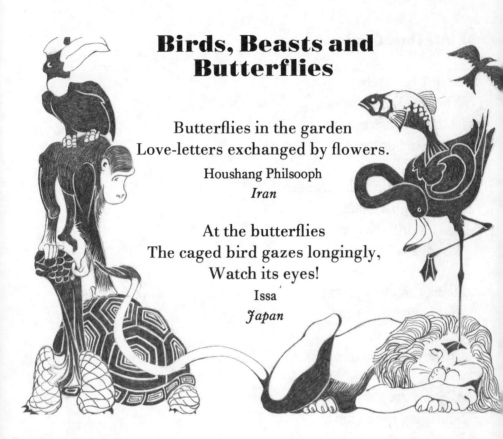

Butterflies in the garden
Love-letters exchanged by flowers.

Houshang Philsooph
Iran

At the butterflies
The caged bird gazes longingly,
Watch its eyes!

Issa
Japan

31 **Butterfly**

Fluttering
From here to yonder
And back again
And across;
Then, zigzaggedly
Landing here and there,
Whispering,
Collecting messages,
The ears of flowers blushing;

Bright colours
Spring
'Mongst bright colours;
In beauty flitting
From one place to next,
Fluttering,
Flittering.

M. P. Alladin
Caribbean

32 In the Garden

Two ink-blue butterflies,
Their probosces curled,
Slumber on a sunflower
Like moored yachts
In a quiet harbour
With gaudy sails unfurled.

A great bumble-bee goes humming by
Like a Zeppelin in the sky,
Encasing the night in each eye.

Rupendra Guha Majumdar
India

33 Adventure

The moon said:
'I will show you gardens more lavish than the sun's;
Flowers more magical;
Stranger enchantments; heavier odours.
Come.'

And the butterfly followed
Down to a distant sea;
And perished
Trying to perch on the foaming blossoms
Of moonlit waves.

Louis Untermeyer
U.S.A.

34 A Fly

If I could
See this fly
With unprejudiced eye,
I should see his body
Was metallic blue – no,
Peacock blue.
His wings are a frosty puff;
His legs fine wire.
He even has a face,
I notice.
And he breathes as I do.

Ruth Dallas
New Zealand

35 The Butterfly

There is no story behind it.
It is split like a second.
It hinges around itself.

It has no future.
It is pinned down to no past.
It's a pun on the present.

It's a little yellow butterfly.
It has taken these wretched hills
under its wings.

Just a pinch of yellow,
it opens before it closes
and closes before it o

where is it

Arun Kolatkur
India

I'm a Parrot

I'm a parrot
I live in a cage
I'm nearly always
in a vex-up rage

I used to fly
all light and free
in the luscious
green forest canopy

I'm a parrot
I live in a cage
I'm nearly always
in a vex-up rage

I miss the wind
against my wing
I miss the nut
and the fruit picking

I'm a parrot
I live in a cage
I'm nearly always
in a vex-up rage

I squawk I talk
I curse I swear
I repeat the things
I shouldn't hear

I'm a parrot
I live in a cage
I'm nearly always
in a vex-up rage

So don't come near me
or put out your hand
because I'll pick you
if I can

     pickyou
     pickyou
     if I can

I want to be free
CAN'T YOU UNDERSTAND
                                     Grace Nichols
                                           U.K.

37 **The Parrot**

The parrot is a thief.
No word
Is safe in earshot
Of that bird.

He picks it up.
He turns it round.
He croaks.
He tries it out for sound.

And then he says it,
Loud and clear,
And all the neighbours
Know you swear.

Edward Lucie-Smith

U.K.

38 **Sparrows at Tea**

This afternoon at four o'clock, in the
      breakfast-room
At the small round table seated, we two
Returning from our seabathe hungry, whom
      The waves have buffeted, without ado
Set to work. The sunlight steps
      Across the doorway; two sparrows follow.
One perches on a chair, the other hops
      Around; both waiting. The cheese is mellow
And the biscuits crisp. The gentian blue
      Teacups are emptied and filled again;
No words are spoken by us two.
      Only the expectant sparrows complain:
They flutter about the room, the whir
      Of their wings enormous in the cosy air;
Then back to the sunlit threshold, confer
      Excitedly, watching us gorging there.

Frank Collymore

Caribbean

The Swallow

The swallow lying curled up on the pavement
had its wings encrusted with tar
and it could not fly. Gina,
who tended it, loosened the clots
with cotton wool soaked in oil
and perfume; she combed its feathers
and hid it in a little basket just
big enough for it to breathe in.
It looked at her almost gratefully
with only one eye. The other
didn't open.
It ate half a leaf of lettuce
and two grains of rice, then slept
for a long time. The following day at dawn
it flew off without saying good-bye.
The maid on the floor above saw it.
What a hurry it was in, was the comment.
And to think that we had saved it from the cats.
But perhaps now it can look after itself.

Engenio Montale
Translated by G. Singh
Italy

40 stretched out
    on the grass
    minding my business –
    this bird, SPLAT!
    right on my head

Ishikawa Takuboku
Translated by C. Sesar
Japan

41 **Cat**

    To plan plan to create to have
    whiskers cool carat silver ready and curved
    bristling

    to plan plan to create to have
    eyes green doors that dilate greenest
    pouncers

    to be ready rubber ball ready
    feet bouncers cool fluid in
    tension

    to be steady steady claws all
    attention to wait wait and create
    pouncing

    to be a cat eeling through alleys
    slipping through windows of odours
    to feel swiftness slowly

to halt at the gate hearing
unlocking whispers paper feet wrapping
potatoes and papers

to hear nicely mice spider feet
scratching great horny nails
catching a fire flies wire legs etch-

ing yet stretching beyond this arch
untriumphant lazily rubb-
ing the soft fur of home

Edward Kamau Brathwaite
Caribbean

42 Cat in the Dark

Look at that!
Look at that!

But when you look
there's no cat.

Without a purr
just a flash of fur
and gone
like a ghost.

The most
you see
are two tiny
green traffic lights
staring at the night.

John Agard
U.K.

43 Cat Out

I let the cat out, peace in her hesitation
against the sharp breeze through the fuchsias.
How, suddenly it becomes so simple to exist
with the freedom of feet and a thick fur.

Taner Baybars
Cyprus

44 **The Dog**

On the roof of a farmhouse,
without respite
the dog
barked at the moon
with red-hot eyes;
at last darkness prevailed
the dog slept
happy to think
he scared the moon far
from the skies.

Anton Buttigieg
Translated by F. Ebejer
Malta

45 from **The Empty Distance Carries**

From the sparkling hills
Comes out the fox in the morning
But when it moves
All the leaves rustle.

Mundari (traditional)
Translated by Sitakant Mahapatra
India

46   from **Our Casuarina Tree**

When first my casement is wide open thrown
    At dawn, my eyes delighted on it rest;
    Sometimes, and most in winter, – on its crest
A grey baboon sits statue-like alone
    Watching the sunrise; while on lower boughs
His puny offspring leap about and play.

Toru Dutt
India

46

Birth of the Foal

May was opening the rosebuds,
elder and lilac beginning to bloom,
it was time for the mare to foal.
She'd rest herself, or hobble lazily

after the boy who sang as he led her
to pasture, wading through the meadow flowers.
They wandered back at dusk, bone-tired
the moon perched on a blue shoulder of sky.

Then the mare lay down,
sweating and trembling, on her straw in the stable.
The drowsy, heavy-bellied cows
surrounded her, waiting, watching, shuffling.

Later, when even the hay slept
and the shaft of the Plough pointed south,
the foal was born. Hours the mare
spent licking the foal with its glue-blind eyes.

And the foal slept at her side
a heap of feathers ripped from a bed.
Straw never spread as soft as this.
Milk or straw never slept like a foal.

Dawn bounced up in a bright red hat,
waved at the world and slipped away.
Up staggered the foal,
its hooves were jelly-knots of foam.

Then day sniffed with its blue nose
through the open stable window, and found them —
the foal nuzzling its mother,
velvet fumbling for her milk.

Then all the trees were talking at once,
chickens scrabbled in the yard,
like golden flowers
envy withered the last stars.

Ferenc Juhasz
Translated by D. Wevill
Hungary

48   The deer on pine mountain,
Where there are no falling leaves,
Knows the coming of autumn
Only by the sound of his own voice.

Onakatomi No Yoshinobu
Translated by K. Rexroth
Japan

49 The Cat-Eyed Owl

The cat-eyed owl, although so fierce
At night with kittens and with mice

In daylight may be mobbed
By flocks of little birds, and in
The market-place, be robbed

Of all his dignity and wisdom
By children market-women and malingering men

Who hoot at it and mocking its myopic
Eyes, shout: 'Look!
Look at it now, he hangs his head in
Shame.' This never happens to the eagle
Or the nightingale.

Edward Kamau Brathwaite

Caribbean

50 The Peasant's Address to His Ox

O Ox, our goodly puller of the plough
Please humour us by pulling straight, and kindly
Do not get the furrows crossed.
Lead the way, O leader, gee-up!
We stooped for days on end to harvest your fodder.
Allow yourself to try just a little, dearest provider.
While you are eating, do not fret about the furrows: eat!
For your stall, O protector of the family
We carried the tons of timber by hand. We
Sleep in the damp, you in the dry. Yesterday
You had a cough, beloved pacemaker.
We were beside ourselves. You won't
Peg out before the sowing, will you, you dog?

Bertolt Brecht
from an Egyptian Peasant's Song 1400 B.C.

Germany

The Magnificent Bull

My bull is white like the silver fish in the river,
White like the shimmering crane bird on the river
   bank
White like fresh milk!
His roar is like thunder to the Turkish cannon
   on the steep shore.
My bull is dark like the raincloud in the storm.
He is like summer and winter.
Half of him is dark like the storm cloud
Half of him is light like sunshine.
His back shines like the morning star.
His brow is red like the back of the hornbill.
His forehead is like a flag, calling the people from
   a distance.
He resembles the rainbow.

I will water him at the river,
With my spear I shall drive my enemies.
Let them water their herds at the well;
The river belongs to me and my bull.
Drink, my bull, from the river; I am here
to guard you with my spear.

from the Dinka
Africa

Oh Taste and Hear!

When eating bamboo sprouts,
remember the man who planted them.

traditional
China

Befoe good food spwile,
nyam till belly buss!

Barbara Zencraft
Caribbean

52 Look!

Look at the sunlight
shaking patterns
through the trees

Look at the raindrops
cupped cool green
in cassava leaves

Look at the bananas
turning
nice and fat and ripe

Look at the watermelon —
how about
a sweet mouth-watering red slice

Grace Nichols
U.K.

53 Sugarcane

When I take
a piece of sugarcane
and put it to me mouth
I does suck and suck
till all the juice come out.

I don't care
if is sun or rain
I does suck and suck
till all the juice come out.

But when I doing homewuk
and same time playing bout
Granny does tell me,
'How you can work properly
and play at the same time?
You brain can't settle.
I always telling you
you can't suck cane and whistle,
you can't suck cane and whistle!'

John Agard
U.K.

All kind o' breadfruit, pumpkin, potato and melon,
Banana, mango, paw-paw and lemon;
Men drinking beer and stout;
Children running all about;
Women licking off duh mout';
And I hungry luk a dog.

Conkies, corn pone, sweet bread selling;
Pork chop, fish cake, souse and puddin';
Women licking off duh mout';
Children running all about;
Men drinking beer and stout;
And I hungry luk a dog.

Fish cutters, beef cutters, rice and stew;
Eddoe soup, pea soup, meal-corn cou-cou;
Children running all about;
Men drinking beer and stout;
Women licking off duh mout';
And I hungry luk a dog.

Peanut, pineapple, patties and plums;
Turn-overs, mauby, ginger beer and rum;
Men drinking beer and stout;
Women licking off duh mout';
Children running all about;
And I hungry luk a dog.

Raw food, cook food, all kind o' food;
Food enough for a multitude;
Women drinking beer and stout;
Men licking off duh mout';
Children running all about;
And I starving.

Glyne Walrond
Caribbean

Sunny Market Song

1st Voice: Coffee
Spiced chocolate
Ackee

White yam
Yellow yam
Juicy melon

Breadfruit
Grapefruit
Arrowroot

2nd Voice: I want some cinnamon and tamarind, mam

3rd Voice: Buy quatty wo't' noh, gal –
Buy quatty wo't'

1st Voice: Tapioca
Sarsaparilla
Cassava

Snapper fish
Fresh fish
Strong charcoal

Dry coconuts
Water coconuts
Mango

2nd Voice: I want some cloves and lemon, mam

3rd Voice: Buy quatty wo't' noh, gal —
Buy quatty wo't'

1st Voice: Custard apple
Ripe pineapple
Sweet potatoes

Cho-cho
Callalu
Coco

Soursop
Sweetsop
Sorrel

2nd Voice: I want some nutmeg and ginger, mam

3rd Voice: Buy quatty wo't' noh, gal —
Buy quatty wo't'

1st Voice: Foo-foo plantain
Ripe plantain
Pawpaw

Fever grass
Strong-back herb
Mount'n honey comb

Orange
Cabbage
Hominy corn

2nd Voice: I want some allspice and pepper, mam

3rd Voice: Buy quatty wo't' noh, gal –
Buy quatty wo't'

1st Voice: Fresh whelks
Beeswax
Floor dye

Blackeye peas
Congo peas
Okra

Jackass rope
Raw sugar
Ripe bananas

2nd Voice: I want some scallion and annatto, mam

3rd Voice: Buy quatty wo't' noh, gal –
Buy quatty wo't'

James Berry
U.K.

For performance: 1st Voice represents general market voices,
2nd Voice represents girl buying spices and seasoning from
3rd Voice, the stallholder.

from **Me Memba Wen**

Me memba wen we use to be ena 4H club a school
We use to get bees, pigs, rabbit, fowl, goat,
An all dem tings de fe look after,
One day, more dan all
We a look after de bees, so we tek out
Some honey fe eat,
One a dem bwoy no mek sure im
Smoke off all de bees,
Im bite de honey comb wid bees pon da
De bees bite im ina in mout
Im bawl out WOH, WOH, mi mout, mi mout
An spit out de whole a it.

Wen we go all a wood bush, we roast
Breadfruit an eat wid pear,
We eat quava, tinken toe, jimbilin,
Sweet cup, custard apple,
So till de whole a dem clide me,
We have sweet sap, sour sap, sweet cup,
Gragefruit, jack fruit, tamarind,
Den we boil jackfruit seed ina black pan.
Bwoy dem da days use to sweet.

Frederick Williams
Caribbean

57   I LOVE THE
friday night
smell of
mammie baking
bread ———— creeping
up to me in
bed, and tho
zzzz I'll fall
asleep, before i
even get a
bite —— when
morning come,
you can bet
I'll meet a
kitchen table
laden with
bread, still
warm and fresh
salt bread
sweet bread
crisp and brown
& best of all
coconut buns
THAT's why
I love the
friday night

smell of mammie
baking bread
putting me to
sleep, dreaming
of jumping from
the highest branch
of the jamoon tree
into the red water
creek
beating calton
run & catching
the biggest fish
in the world
plus, getting
the answers right
to every single
sum
that every day
in my dream
begins and ends
with the friday
night smell of
mammie baking
bread, and
coconut buns
of course.

Marc Matthews
Caribbean

58 Yam

Yam, yam, yam,
You are of pure white.
You have a gown of meat.
You have a cap of vegetables,
You have trousers of fish.
Yam, oh yam, oh yam.

from the Yoruba
Translated by U. Beier
Africa

59 Fingerlicking

I went to the kitchen
Find de food finger licking
I tek out a de fridge
A nice big piece a chicken.
I started to nyam it
But me mammy come an grab it
And gimme a piece a licking
And sen me to me bed.

Judith Ellis
U.K.

60 O rhinoceros, O man rhinoceros,
Rhinoceros of the river banks
Is good to eat with tomatoes.

from the Chikunda
Translated by R. Finnegan
Africa

61 **Gold**

The woman touches her bun
of thinning hair. She laughs,
and drops a spoon and a hunk of bread
in their reaching, grubby hands.
Like roses divining water
the circle of thin red necks
leans over the steaming plates;
red noses bloom in the savoury mist.

The stars of their eyes shine
like ten worlds lost in their own light.
In the soup, slowly circling
swim golden onion rings.

Ferenc Juhasz
Translated by D. Wevill
Hungary

Marigold Pie

'Say what you will,
You won't pass by
If you can't make a
Marigold pie.'

'Let me pass!
I don't lie
And I can make a
Marigold pie.'

'Marigold petals.
Two small stones,
Lawn-grass clippings,
Chicken bones,
A spider's web with one dead fly
All mixed up in the wink of an eye.
And here it is for you to try.'

'Thanks, but no thanks – pass on by.'

Dennis Doyle
U.K.

Nightscapes

Look at the cloud-cat lapping there on high
With lightening tongue the moon-milk
from the sky!
Kalidasa
India

What is day to the bat
is night to the crow.

Ghuhum Hasan Beg Arif
India

Evening

In the woods full of evening the nightingales are silent
The rivers absorb the sky and its fountains
Birds return to the indigo shores from the shadows
A scarlet pearl of sunshine in their beaks.

Ahmet Hasim
Translated by N. Menemencioglu
Turkey

64   from **We Have Come Home**

The gurgling drums
Echo the stars
The forest howls
And between the trees
The dark sun appears.

Lenrie Peters
Africa

65   **At Night**

When the tide comes in
and the moon
comes out,
the sea goes to bed
and all is still
as still as can be

Even the fish
sense the still
and quietly sliver
in between the rocks
and seek a place
for night.

The whole world of sea
seems to rest at night.
Even the little waves
creep silently upon
the shore.

Raymond McCormack*
Australia

66 **Night**

Silently sleeps the river.
The dark pines hold their peace.
The nightingale does not sing,
Or the corncrake screech.

Night. Silence enfolds.
Only the brook murmurs,
And the brilliant moon turns
Everything to silver.

Silver the river,
And the rivulets.
Silver the grass
Of the fertile steppes.

Night. Silence enfolds.
All sleeps in Nature
And the brilliant moon
Turns everything to silver.

Sergei Esenin
Translated by G. Thurley
Russia

67 Bed

I get into bed
I am an ice-block but
I soon melt.

I lie there tossing my
Thoughts
And, like a bird
I flutter to sleep.

David Recht*
Australia

68 The Moon

The moon lights the earth
it lights the earth but still
the night must remain the night.
The night cannot be like the day.
The moon cannot dry our washing.
Just like a woman cannot be a man
just like black can never be white.

from the Soussou
Translated by U. Beier
Africa

69 The Moon

The moon cannot fight
Sun leave him alone.
The moon cannot fight
Sun leave him alone!

The moon gives the earth his good light.
Come and eat bean cakes with us at midnight.
Thief! Thief with the goggle eye!

from the Yoruba
Translated by U. Beier
Africa

70 Four Moons

The cowboy's moon is thin and clear,
A lazy C on a midnight steer.

Robin Hood's moon lets planets go
Like burning arrows from his bow.

Over the sea the pirate's moon
Glitters like a gold doubloon.

But the spaceman's moon is round and white
Like a porthole on the side of night.

Dennis Doyle
U.K.

71 Only the Moon

When I was a child I thought
The new moon was a cradle
The full moon was granny's round face.

The new moon was a banana
The full moon was a big cake.

When I was a child
I never saw the moon
I only saw what I wanted to see.

And now I see the moon
It's the moon
Only the moon, and nothing but the moon.

Wong May
Translated by E. Thumboo
Singapore

72 Moonlight

I saw moonlight lying on the ground,
I stooped and touched the ground with my hand.
And found it was common earth,
Dust was in my palm.

P. J. Chaudhury
India

73 Fear

Curling fingers
crawling up
the back
of your
brain,
taking your mind
by
surprise,
then gripping
your heart and
squeezing it
of it's
life source.
A plunger
pushing
the contents
of your
stomach
down and
out.

Deepak Kalha*
U.K.

I Like to Stay Up

I like to stay up
and listen
when big people talking
jumbie stories

Ooooooooooooooooooh
I does feel so tingly
and excited
inside — eeeeeeeeeeee

But when my mother say
'Girl, time for bed'
then is when
I does feel a dread
then is when
I does jump into me bed
then is when
I does cover up
from me feet to me head

then is when
I does wish
I didn't listen
to no stupid jumbie story
then is when
I does wish
I did read me book instead

Grace Nichols
U.K.

Song of the Fishing Ghosts

Night is the time when phantoms play,
   Flows the river,
   Phantoms white
   Phantoms black
Fish in the dark salt water bay.

Skulls are nets for phantom fishers,
   Flows the river,
Phantoms red on a phantom river
   Dark flows the river.

Black phantom splashes
   Flows the river
White phantom splashes
   Flows the river.

Night is the time when phantoms play,
   Heads are nets
   For phantom fishers
There on the dark salt water bay.

   Phantoms black
   Phantoms red
   Phantoms white
   For nets their heads
And the dark, dark, dark river flows.

Efua Sutherland
Africa

76   The Mystery of Darkness

The mystery of darkness
Lies in its blackness
The beauty of blackness
Lies in its rhythm
So listen to the rhythm
The rhythm of blackness
And hear the voices
The voices of darkness
LOVE . . . the beauty of blackness
RESPECT . . . the mystery of darkness
HEAR . . . the voices of darkness
AND MOVE . . . to the rhythm of blackness

Lari Williams
Africa

77   The Stars are Thundering

The stars are thundering in the sky.
Among the ant-hills the cobra roars.
Under the earth the cobra's mate is nodding,
And the eagle dances across the sky.

Gond (traditional)
Translated by R. Finnegan
India

78 Calligram

The sky's as blue and black as ink
My eyes drown in it and sink

Darkness a shell whines over me
I write this under a willow tree

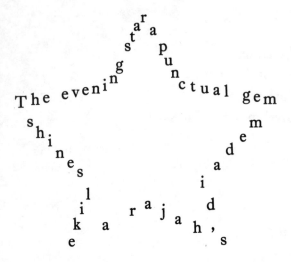

Guillaume Apollinaire
Translated by O. Bernard
France

79 A Dream

In the cold boughs brushing the sky
a couple of stars are hung
like dust,
like splinters of glass.

Kaoru Maruyama
Translated by I. Kono
Japan

80 **The Day Has Gone**

The Day has gone and the Night
has come
Go to sleep
my little one

Dream Dream Dream
about me Dream
about the lovely things
you see

Dream about the flower
don't Dream about the bee
it might sting you.

Accabre Huntley*
U.K.

81 from **The Waters of Sleep**

For here by the cool river,
Icy cold, the north wind blows and rustles
The apple trees. Then, through the leaves, comes falling
Sleep's cool cataract.

Sappho, 500 B.C.
Translated by B. Saklatuala
Greece

Cock Crow Song

In the eastern quarter dawn breaks, the stars
flicker pale.
The morning cock at Nu-nan mounts the wall and
crows.
The songs are over, the clock run down, but
still the feast is set.
The moon grows dim and the stars are few; morning has come to the world.
At a thousand gates and ten thousand doors the
fish-shaped keys turn;
Round the Palace and up by the Castle, the crows
and magpies are flying.

1st Century B.C.
Translated by A. Waley
China

Songs and Stories

The children   Why do you go so far
from the little square?

Myself   I go in search of magicians
and of princesses.

Garcia Lorca
Spain

If you can walk
you can dance
If you can talk
you can sing

traditional
Zimbabwe

83   Tell me a story
With knights and princesses,
With horses and helmets
And long velvet dresses;
With dwarves in the forest
And kings in the palace –
A story that we could
Step into like Alice
Through magical mirrors
Our weight would not crack,
To live in that country   Dennis Doyle
And never come back.   *U.K.*

Gaily bedight,
A gallant knight,
In sunshine and in shadow,
Had journeyed long,
Singing a song,
In search of Eldorado.

But he grew old —
This knight so bold
And o'er his heart a shadow
Fell as he found
No spot of ground
That looked like Eldorado.

And, as his strength
Failed him at length,
He met a pilgrim shadow —
'Shadow', said he,
'Where can it be —
This land of Eldorado?'

'Over the Mountains
Of the Moon,
Down the Valley of the Shadow,
Ride, boldly ride,'
The shade replied,
'If you seek for Eldorado!'

Edgar Allan Poe
U.S.A.

The Raven Ralph

The Raven Ralph
    will will hoo hoo,
he halped himsalf
    still still do do
all on his own
at Raven's Stone
    will will still still
        hoo hoo.

The Maid of Mist
    will will hoo hoo
knows every twist
    still still do do
'Take, take,' said she,
'tis all for free.'
Will will still still
        hoo hoo.

But when at last
    will will hoo hoo
a year had passed
    still still do do
the sun rose red
and Ralph lay dead
    will will still still
        do do.

Christian Morgenstern
Translated by M. Knight
Germany

The Herd Boy's Song

Splashing water,
Luscious grass,
Somebody's child is herding an ox,
Riding his ox by the river-side.
Browsing ox,
Happy youth.
Somebody's child is singing a song,
Shouting his song to a little white cloud;

> Away at morn my ox I ride,
> And back again at eventide.

> My two feet never touch the dust;
> In wealth and fame who puts his trust?

> My rush hat shelters me from rain,
> In silk and sables what's the gain?

> I quench my thirst at a mountain-rill;
> Who'd spend a fortune his belly to fill?

> When the sun on his golden horse rides high
> Down by the river go ox and I;

> When the sinking sun makes shadows creep
> He carries me home on his back asleep.

Chen Shan-Shih
Translated by R. C. Trevelyan
China

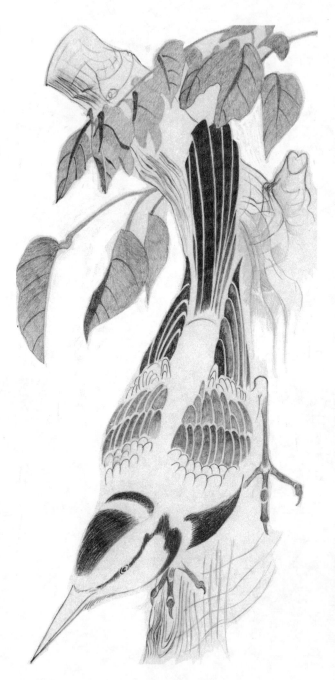

Woodpecker

Carving
tap/tap
music
out of
tap/tap
tree trunk
keep me
busy
whole day
tap/tap
long

tap/tap
pecker
birdsong
tap/tap
pecker
birdsong

tree bark
is tap/tap
drumskin
fo me beak
I keep
tap/tap
rhythm
fo forest
heartbeat

tap/tap
chisel beak
long
tap/tap
honey leak
song
pecker/tap
tapper/peck
pecker
birdsong

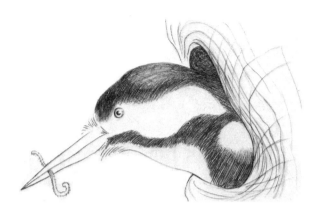

John Agard
U.K.

88 **Cradle Song**

From groves of spice
O'er fields of rice,
Athwart the lotus-stream,
    I bring for you,
    Aglint with dew
A little lovely dream.

    Sweet, shut your eyes
    The wild fire-flies
Dance through the fairy neem:
    From the poppy-bole
    For you I stole
A little lovely dream.

Dear eyes, good night,
In golden light
The stars around you gleam;
On you I press
With soft caress
A little lovely dream.

Sarojini Naidu
India

89 Workings of the Wind

Wind doesn't always topple trees
and shake houses to pieces.

Wind plays
all over woods, with weighty ghosts
in swings in thousands,
swinging from every branch.

Wind doesn't always rattle windows
and push, push at walls.

Wind whistles
down cul-de-sacs and worries
dry leaves and old newspapers to leap
and curl like kite tails.

Wind doesn't always dry out
sweaty shirts and blouses.

Wind scatters
pollen dust of flowers, washes
people's and animals' faces
and combs out birds' feathers.

Wind doesn't always whip up waves
into white horses.

Wind shakes up
tree-shadows to dance on rivers,
to jig about on grass, and hanging
lantern light to play signalman.

Wind doesn't always run wild
kicking tinny dustbin lids.

Wind makes
leafy limbs bow to red roses
and bob up and down outside windows
and makes desk papers fly up indoors.

James Berry
U.K.

90 **Ballad of Sixty-Five**

The roads are rocky and the hills are steep,
The macca stretches and the gully's deep.
The town is far, news travels slow.
And the mountain men have far to go.

Bogle took his cutlass at Stony Gut
And looked at the small heap of food he'd got
And he shook his head, and his thoughts were sad,
'You can wuk like a mule but de crop still bad.'

Bogle got his men and he led them down
Over the hills to Spanish Town,
They chopped their way and they made a track
To the Governor's house. But he sent them back.

As they trudged back home to Stony Gut
Paul's spirit sank with each bush he cut,
For he thought of the hungry St. Thomas men
Who were waiting for the message he'd bring to them.

They couldn't believe that he would fail
And their anger rose when they heard his tale.
Then they told Paul Bogle of Morant Bay
And the poor man fined there yesterday.

Then Bogle thundered, 'This thing is wrong.
They think we weak, but we hill men strong.
Rouse up yourself. We'll march all night
To the Vestry house, and we'll claim our right.'

The Monday morning was tropic clear
As the men from Stony Gut drew near,
Clenching their sticks in their farmer's hand
To claim their rights in their native land.

Oh many mourned and many were dead
That day when the vestry flames rose red.
There was chopping and shooting and when it done
Paul Bogle and the men knew they had to run.

They ran for the bush where they hoped to hide
But the soldiers poured in from Kingston side.
They took their prisoners to Morant Bay
Where they hanged them high in the early day.

Paul Bogle died but his spirit talks
Anywhere in Jamaica that freedom walks,
Where brave men gather and courage thrills
As it did in those days in St. Thomas hills.

Alma Norman
Caribbean

91 Limbo

And limbo stick is the silence in front of me
limbo

limbo
limbo like me
limbo
limbo like me

long dark night is the silence in front of me
limbo
limbo like me

stick hit sound
and the ship like it ready

stick hit sound
and the dark still steady

limbo
limbo like me

long dark deck and the water surrounding me
long dark deck and the silence is over me

limbo
limbo like me

stick is the whip
and the dark deck is slavery

stick is the whip
and the dark deck is slavery

limbo
limbo like me

drum stick knock
and the darkness is over me

knees spread wide
and the water is hiding me

limbo
limbo like me

knees spread wide
and the dark ground is under me

down
down
down

and the drummer is calling me

limbo
limbo like me

sun coming up
and the drummers are praising me

out of the dark
and the dumb gods are raising me

up
up
up

and the music is saving me

hot
slow
step

on the burning ground.

Edward Kamau Brathwaite
Caribbean

The flowers are finished
So is my song
Accept my last offering, Lord.

Rabindranath Tagore
India

Glossary of Dialect Words

This glossary is intended as a rough guide for readers unfamiliar with Caribbean dialect. Many of the poems are based on an oral, folk tradition and literal translations cannot always be made. The best way to get the sense of a poem is to read it aloud.

Spellings of dialect words may vary from poem to poem.

a – is, I, me, at, of
ackee – fruit
anedda – another
annatto – tree whose berries are
  used for dye
befoe – before
bessis – best
bredda – brother
bruk – broke
buss – burst
bwoy – boy

callalu – edible leaves, greens
calton – Carlton (a boy's name)
cassava – staple food
chocho – climbing vine eaten as a
  vegetable
clide – full up, satisfied (with food)
coco – coconut
corn pone – cakes made of maize
  or wheat
cou cou – soup

da – that, at, in, on, to
dan – than
dat – that
de – the
deh, dey – there
dem – they, them, those

eddoe – yam
eena, ena, ina – in
ehn, ehen – even

fe, fi – for, to
foo foo, fu fu – mashed food, stew,
  soup, etc.

gadda – gather
gat – got
git – get

he – his, he is
hep – help

im – him
im a comme – he's coming

jackass rope – rope made out of twisted tobacco leaves
jap – wasp
jimbilin – fruit
jumbie – ghost

'kin – skin

lib – live
lick – hit
liddung – lie, lying, lay down
likkle – little
luk – like

macca – tarmac road
manby – locally brewed drink
me – I
memba – remember
mek – make
mi – my
mout – mouth

neem – tree
nite – night
no – no, not any, won't you, isn't that so?
nyam – eat

o – of
odda – other
okra – vegetable
ow – how

pon – upon

quatty – penny and a half

sen – send
solja – soldier
soursop – fruit
spwile – spoil
sweetsop – fruit

tan – remain
teck, tek – take
ting – thing
todder, todda – the other
tousan – thousand

wen – when
wid – with
wo't' noh – won't you now
wuk – work

yeye – eye(s)
yu, yuh – you

Solutions to riddles

Two tiny birds . . . trees	*(eyes)*
The black one . . . bottom	*(cooking pot and fire)*
A round calabash . . . grass	*(moon and stars)*
A thin staff . . . earth	*(rain)*
You cannot . . . feather	*(your breath)*
Here's a thing . . . one a-stare	*(the face)*

List of Poets Categorised by Nationality

Africa
Okot p'Bitek
Lenrie Peters
Efua Sutherland
Lari Williams
Chikunda/traditional
Dinka/traditional
Igbo/traditional
Soussou/traditional
Yoruba/traditional

Australia
Ross Falconer*
Raymond McCormack*
David Recht*

Canada
Dennis Lee

Caribbean
M. P. Alladin
Edward Kamau Brathwaite
Frank Collymore
Paul Keens-Douglas
Marc Matthews
Alma Norman
Odette Thomas
Glyne Walrond
Frederick Williams
Barbara Zencraft

China
Chen Shan-Shih
traditional proverbs translated by H. Hart
anon. translated by A. Waley

Cyprus
Taner Baybars

France
Guillaume Apollinaire

Germany
Bertolt Brecht
Christian Morgenstern

Greece
Kassia translated by P. Diehl
Sappho

Hong Kong
Chun Po Man

Hungary
Ferenc Juhasz

India
Ghuhum Hasan Beg Arif
P. J. Chaudhury
Toru Dutt
Kalidasa translated by J. Brough
Arun Kolatkur
Rupendra G. Majumdar

Sarojini Naidu
Rabindranath Tagore
Gond/traditional
Mundari/traditional

Iran
Houshang Philsooph

Italy
Eugenio Montale

Japan
Issa translated by H. Henderson
Kaoru Maruyama
Ishikawa Takuboku
Onakatomi No Yoshinobu

Malta
Anton Buttigieg
anon. translated by A. Arberry

New Zealand
Ruth Dallas

Pakistan
Taufiq Rafat

Russia
Sergei Esenin

Singapore
Wong May
Edwin Thumboo

Spain
Garcia Lorca translated by Spender and Gili

Turkey
Ahmet Hasim

United Kingdom
John Agard
James Berry
Valerie Bloom
Dennis Doyle
Judith Ellis
Prabhu S. Guptara
Beshlie Heron
Marisa Horsford*
Accabre Huntley*
Deepak Kalha*
Edward Lucie-Smith
Lesley Miranda*
H. O. Nazareth
Grace Nichols
Desmond Strachan*
Vivian Usherwood*

U.S.A.
Mary A. Hoberman
Edgar Allan Poe
May Swenson
Louis Untermeyer

Acknowledgements

The editor and publisher would like to thank the following for contributing poems specially for this anthology: Edward Kamau Brathwaite, Lesley Miranda Agard, Grace Nichols, Desmond Strachan, Paul Keens-Douglas, Valerie Bloom, Prabhu S. Guptara, H.O. Nazareth, Marc Matthews, James Berry, John Agard.

We would also like to thank those listed below for permission to reproduce poems: 1,73 from *Tall Thoughts*, Basement Writers; 2,65,67 from *Once Around the Sun* edited by Brian Thompson, Oxford University Press 1966; 3,40 from *Poems to Eat* translated by C Sesar, Ward Lock 1966; 4 from *City Times* edited by Paul Ashton, English Centre 1982; 5,80 from Accabre Huntley *At School Today*, Bogle L'Ouverture Publications Ltd 1977; 6,54 from Glynne Walrond *The Children's Voice*, Arthur H Stockwell Ltd, 1981; 7,42,53 from John Agard *I Din Do Nuttin*, 1983 reprinted by permission of The Bodley Head; 8 from Beshlie Heron *Here Today and Gone Tomorrow*, Broomsleigh Press 1978; 10 from Odette Thomas *Rain Falling, Sun Shining*, Bogle-L'Ouverture Publications Ltd 1975; 11 from Marisa Horsford *Poems*, Your Own Stuff Press 1979; 13 from Vivian Usherwood *Poems*, Centreprise Publications 1975; 14 © Desmond Strachan; 15 from *Tim Tim* by Paul Keens-Douglas; 18 reproduced by permission of OUP from *A Maltese Anthology* compiled by A J Arberry, © OUP 1960; 19 from Okot p'Bitek *Home of my Love*, Heinemann Educational Books 1974; 20 from *Oh Such Foolishness* edited by Cole and Ungerer, published by Russell and Vulkenning; 21 from *Igbo Traditional Verse* edited by R Egudu and N Nwoga reprinted by permission of Heinemann Books; 22,62,70,83 from Denis Doyle, *Apricot Rhymes*, Commonplace Workshop; 23 © 1974 by Dennis Lee, from *Nicholas Knock and other People* by Dennis Lee, reprinted by permission of Macmillan of Canada, a division of Gage Publishing Limited; 28 copyright © 1976 by May Swenson, by permission of Little, Brown and Company in association with the Atlantic Monthly Press; 29 from 'Child's Delight' by Edwin Thumboo, Federal Publications (S) PTE Ltd, Singapore, 1972; 30 from *First Voices* edited by Shahid Hosain, Oxford University Press Pakistan 1965; 31 from M P Alladin, *Monstrous Angel*; 32 from *Indo-English Poetry in Bengal* edited by K C Lahiri, Writer's Workshop, Calcutta 1974; 33 from Louis Untermeyer *Roast Leviathan*, Harcourt Brace & Co, New York 1923; 34 from Ruth Dallas *Shadow Show*, Caxton Press, New Zealand; 35 from *Jejuri* by Arun Kolatkar; 37 copyright © 1970 by Edward Lucie-Smith 39 from E Montale *New Poems* translated by G Singh, Chatto and Windus 1976; 41 reproduced by permission of OUP from Edward Kamau Brathwaite *Other Exiles*, © OUP 1975; 43 from T Baybars *Narcissus in a Dry Pool*, Sidgwick and Jackson 1978; 44 from *Cross Winds* edited by Oliver Friggieri, Wilfion Books; 45 Mundari Song from *The Empty Distance Carries*, translated by Sitakanta Mahapatra, Writer's Workshop, Calcutta 1974; 46 from *Ancient Ballads and Legends of Hindustan*, Kegan Paul and Trench 1882; 47,61 from Sandor Weores and Ferenc Juhasz *Selected poems*, translated by Edwin Morgan and David Wevill, Penguin Modern European Poems 1970, copyright © Ferenc Juhasz 1970, translations and introductions to Ferenc Juhasz copyright © David Wevill 1970, reprinted by permission of Penguin Books Ltd; 48 from Kenneth Rexroth *One Hundred Poems from the Japanese*, All Rights Reserved, reprinted by permission of New Directions Publishing Corporation; 50 from Bertolt Brecht *Poems 1913-1956* translated by Patrick Bridgwater, Methuen 1976; 51 from *African Poetry for Schools*, East African Publishing House 1970; 55 from *A Caribbean Anthology*, ILEA publications © James Berry; 56 from *Me Wemba Wen* © Frederick Williams; 59 from *Black Eye Perceptions* published by Black Ink 1981; 60 reproduced by permission of OUP from R Finnegan *Oral Literature in Africa*, © OUP 1970; 63 from *The Penguin Book of Turkish Verse*, Penguin Books Limited 1978; 64 from Lenrie Peters *Selected Poetry* reprinted by permission of Heinemann Educational Books; 66 from *Confessions of a Hooligan*, fifty poems by Sergei Esenin, translated by Geoffrey Thurley, Carcanet Press Ltd; 71 from *Seven Poets*, Singapore University Press, National University of Singapore; 72 from *Selected Poems of Pj Chaudhury*, Writer's Workshop, Calcutta 1978; 75 from *Messages. Poems from Ghana* edited by K Awoonor and Adali-Mortty, Heinemann Educational Books 1971; 76 from *Drumcall*, Barbican Books 1971; 77 from *The Penguin Book of Oral Poetry* edited by R Finnegan, Allen Lane 1978, reprinted by permission of Penguin Books Ltd; 78 from Apollinaire: *Selected Poems* translated by Oliver Bernard, Penguin Modern European Poets 1965, translation copyright © Oliver Bernard 1954, reprinted by permission of Penguin Books Ltd; 79 from *An Anthology of Modern Japanese Poetry*, edited and translated by Ichiro Kono and Rikutaro Fukuda, Kentyusha Ltd, Tokyo 1957 81 from *Sapho of Lesbos* edited and translated by B Saklatuala, Charles Skilton Ltd 1968; 82 from *One Hundred and Seventy Chinese Poems* edited and translated by A Waley, Constable 1918; 84 from *Poems of E A Poe*, George Bell and Sons; 85 from Christian Morgenstein *Galgenlieder* translated by Max Knight University of California Press 1963; 86 from *The Dragon Book*, William Hodge and Co; 88 from *Indo-English poetry in Bengal* edited by K C Lahiri, Oxford University Press 1945; 90 from *Ballad of Jamaica*, Longman Group Limited; 91 from Edward Kamau Brathwaite *The Arrivants*, © OUP 1973.

Theme epigraphs: page 7 from *The Penguin Book of Women Poets* translated by Patrick Diehl, and *700 Chinese Proverbs* edited and translated by Henry Hart, Stanford University Press 1937. Pages 21 and 52 from Barbara Zencraft *Native Soul* Sangster's Bookstore Jamaica, and *700 Chinese Proverbs* edited and translated by Henry Hart, Stanford University Press 1937. Page 34 thanks to Houshang Philsooph, and from *The Bamboo Broom* translated by H Henderson, Routledge and Kegan Paul. Page 65 from *Poems from the Sansbrit* translated by J Brough (Penguin Classics 1968) Copyright © John Brough 1968. Reprinted by permission of Penguin Books Ltd.

Every effort has been made to reach copyright holders; the publishers would be glad to hear from anyone whose rights they have unknowingly infringed.